GOT IT

THE ANSWER TO A CONFIDENT, PRODUCTIVE AND STRESS-FREE LIFE

Do you have confidence? Are you productive and do you find it easy to just get on with things? Is your life stress-free? Have you got it? If not –this book is for you.

LINDSEY REED

This edition first published 2017

A catalogue record for this book is available from the British Library

ISBN 978-0-9957301-0-6

Type setting: Laura Davies
Publishing: Glows Coaching & Books
Print & Distribution: Ingram Content Group

This book is dedicated to five special men in my life.

If you can dream - and not make dreams your master;
If you can think - and not make thoughts your aim;
If you can meet with Triumph and Disaster
And treat those two impostors just the same;
If you can bear to hear the truth you've spoken
Twisted by knaves to make a trap for fools,
Or watch the things you gave your life to, broken,
And stoop and build 'em up with worn-out tools:

EXTRACT FROM IF, BY RUDYARD KIPLING

Contents

Chapter 1: Looking in the Wrong Place

You have wisdom inside you – listen for it and give it voice.

You have light inside you – feel its glow and let it shine.

You have power inside you – let your wisdom and light guide you as you make things manifest in the world.

MICHAEL NEILL

Chapter 1: Looking in the Wrong Place

I had been looking in the wrong place to find confidence. And I was not alone! So many of us are looking in the wrong place. Yet, when we understand the simple Principles that I will be sharing with you, confidence becomes so easy. How on earth did I miss it? Now that I have realised the secret to true confidence, everything is the same and yet so different...

I have written this book so that you can discover your inner confidence and lead a productive and stress-free life, just as I did. In order that you have an understanding how this book has been created for you, let me share with you where my story began.

Until 2005 I worked in the finance industry as head of operational teams, leading multi-million pound projects. I successfully climbed the career ladder in a male dominated environment and all without a degree. I had been continually told that not having a University education would stop me from becoming a manager, let alone a senior one, but I proved them wrong.

Despite this career success, I was suffering from a severe lack of confidence which I had become very good at hiding. On the outside I appeared calm and confident, but deep inside I was an anxious wreck, constantly feeling that I would be 'found out'. I was on the verge of a nervous breakdown when I reached out for help. And that's when I first experienced professional coaching, and my life was turned around.

I am sharing this with you so that you can see that I have suffered from (and can relate to) confidence issues including experiencing all the things that these can trigger: procrastinating, being a perfectionist, overthinking, worry and stress.

When I left the corporate world, friends and associates began to see a difference in me and asked for advice on their careers. I so enjoyed working with them but sadly noticed that many were also suffering from a lack of confidence. I desperately didn't want people to suffer from the shackles that were holding them back and wanted to find ways to help them release from these. I embarked on studying to be a professional coach, as well as learning all that I could on how to be confident.

Since then I have coached hundreds of business owners and leaders as well as running regular

Confidence Workshops. Initially I used tools and techniques, anchoring states, belief busters, shifting stuck emotions; resulting in many clients having life-changing realisations. Instinctively, I knew that it was all to do with our thinking. In the early days I would focus on the content of people's thinking but clients would get stuck in their own stories. During that time, I certainly developed my listening skills!

I then learnt that listening to the content wasn't particularly helpful. Through my coaching and Neuro Linguistic Programming (NLP) training, I learnt to analyse the structure of thinking. I spent ages learning about filters and the names of language patterns (nominalisations, complex equivalence, modal operators – I even created a spreadsheet of them!) and became competent at spotting these.

And then, by chance - through winning a competition for a free place on a workshop - I discovered something that, I believe, is more impactful than the approaches I have used in the past.

Even though clients got amazing results with the old methods I used, what I am sharing with you in this book is more powerful. This is transformational. I, and many of my clients, have noticed huge shifts that sustain. I have noticed that I am so much more productive, relaxed and have clarity. In addition, clients are confident; problems that they perceived they had, just seem to disappear.

So, what is the secret to finding true confidence?

When we want to fully comprehend how something works, it is best to understand key principles.

Definition of a Principle (Cambridge Dictionary)

A basic idea or rule that explains or controls how something happens or works.

1. **Constant** – it's always true – never varies – even if you don't know / believe it – it is still there

2. **Explanatory** – it explains how something works and provides a complete account of something – there are no anomalies

3. **Predictive** – you can predict the outcome

(Much thanks to Keith Blevens PhD and Valda Monroe for explaining the criteria of a principle.)

For example, when studying maths you need a working knowledge of the basic principles of mathematics such as Pythagoras, scaling, algebra in order to progress and succeed in this subject. And don't we all want to progress and succeed in some way?

What I will be sharing with you are the principles about us as human beings; how we experience what we experience and the mechanics of our thinking.

These are the secrets to finding your true confidence.

Guess what? You already have confidence – you've probably just been looking in the wrong place!

Bad smells are not the answer

Going back in time to the Great Plague of 1665, doctors used to wear masks that looked like duck's bills, filled with dried flowers, herbs and spices. They thought that disease was spread by miasma, a toxic form of 'bad air' (in fact the word malaria comes from, 'bad= mal, air = aria'). They believed that these fresh, sweet smells would protect them from diseases when operating on patients.

The doctors would operate with dirty hands, wearing dirty aprons and reusing dirty knives. Looking back, why would they think of washing their hands and instruments if they believed that disease came from smells, not germs? It all seems quite incredulous now; however, filthy and foul-smelling areas within the poor communities tended to be where epidemics would stem from, explaining why (without science) they came to that conclusion. When housing, sanitation and general cleanliness was improved, this reduced the level of disease. They got a healthier result – but they were still looking in the wrong place.

One person - who by accident was on the right path - was Ignaz Semmelweis, a Hungarian doctor in a maternity clinic. He noticed a vast difference in the survival rate of mothers and babies between the wards that were run by doctors, and those that were run by midwives. The key difference was that doctors were dissecting and operating on diseased bodies whereas midwives focused on delivering babies.

He tried to investigate what specifically prevented the deaths. Through trial and error, Semmelweis discovered that when all doctors and midwives rigorously washed their hands with chlorine solution, the number of fatalities was reduced considerably.

Sadly (and possibly due to his untactful approach by berating the profession) his method was not adopted so women and children continued to lose their lives.

It wasn't until scientists discovered germs and convinced people of the importance of hygiene that the death rate began to reduce dramatically. Medics and scientists had been looking in the wrong place; it wasn't bad smells but microorganisms that caused disease.

You Can't Smell Confidence...

Like disease, confidence cannot be smelt! It can't be seen, or touched.

Similar to the doctors, I was simply looking for confidence in all the wrong places. I knew that confidence was to do with our thinking. I knew that it wasn't to do with our past either – our thinking was just interpreting this. I knew that it wasn't to do with external influences or environment. I was so close... and yet so far! I read books, attended workshops, asked questions and even had my own coaches trying to figure out the secret to confidence.

Then, as I mentioned earlier, I won a competition and attended a three day workshop – and life changed!

What I have discovered since then is a deep understanding of *being human* which has given me a sense of peace and contentment. I don't get annoyed or flair up with irritation like I used to. All my insecurities have disappeared. I feel more creative and energetic than ever. Life seems so much easier and more joyful. I am forever grateful for stumbling upon this learning and cannot wait to share this with you and others around the world.

Let's get started!

Chapter 2: No Tips or Techniques here

Our ordinary mind always tries to persuade us that we are nothing but acorns and that our greatest happiness will be to become bigger, fatter, shinier acorns; but that is of interest only to pigs. Our faith gives us knowledge of something better: that we can become oak trees.

E.F. SCHUMACHER

Chapter 2: No Tips or Techniques here

I have written this book because I personally have benefitted hugely from what I am about to share with you, and so have clients and many others around the world. However I believe the numbers are too small.

My vision is to create harmony and joy in this world and touch millions of people's lives, enabling them to recognise and be their extraordinary selves and for them to then pass this learning on to others. And this is what I wish for you.

Struggling with confidence and stress prevents us from being extra-ordinary. So we need to start with ourselves – as the popular quote states:

Be the change that you wish to see in the world

By shifting your mind-set, you can be your best self, be an inspiring leader in your own way, *and be extraordinary*. And by tapping into your amazing inner wisdom (which you will discover through reading this book) you also can shape and make waves in the world if you so wish.

You may be a business owner, a leader, a parent… whoever you are, you will benefit from reading this.

Lack of confidence, busy-ness and stress affects many people around the world. You are certainly not alone.

Can you relate to any of the following?

- ☐ Do you feel a fraud and not really as good as people think? Do you think that you will be 'found out'?
- ☐ Do you hate being pushed into the limelight and prefer to hide in the background or put on a false façade, hoping that your insecurities won't be noticed?
- ☐ Are you constantly feeling worried and anxious, fearing the unknown, failure or success?
- ☐ Do you feel angered by the unfairness of life and blame others for your lack of confidence?
- ☐ Do you avoid social and networking situations, as you can never think of anything to say?
- ☐ Are you struggling with relationship issues, breakdown or loss?
- ☐ Do you suffer from overthinking and find that your mind never stops?
- ☐ Do you waste time procrastinating or being a perfectionist?
- ☐ Do you feel stressed and as a result, your health is suffering?

Whatever brought you here, the very fact that you are

reading this book means that now is the right time for something to change in your life.

As well as confidence, this book will help you if you suffer from a busy, overactive mind. Perhaps 'busy' is a word that you often use! Does your work often overtake your life and leave you feeling distracted and detached – even when you are with family and friends? Do you find issues difficult to resolve, making your head spin and trapping you in the thick of it, unable to find clarity? Do you come away from meetings, networking and social functions berating yourself and feeling insecure?

Perhaps money is an issue and if you are a business owner, do you find it difficult to charge what you are worth and have even avoided following up on potential opportunities?

I relate to all of the above – I've been there, done that and got the t-shirt!

I remember years ago a very dear friend was on holiday and found a t-shirt that she nearly bought for me. It had a cartoon cat on the front looking scared with the words "I thrive on stress".

The universal principles I am about to share will free you up from this. By the end of the book, you will experience:

- Naturally feeling confident and feeling at peace
- Having a clear mind and clarity; decisions become easy to make
- Extra energy, allowing you to be more productive
- Seeing life with a lighter perspective with balance and a sense of joy
- Enjoying life in the moment, both at work and home. It's far more enriching
- Finding that your anxieties or conflicts are overcome within minutes rather than hours, days or weeks!

There are plenty of books on 'how to' be confident. However this one is different from the norm. There will be no building skills or competencies, no learning step-by-step guides or tips or techniques – there will be no 'how to'. The last thing I want to do is give you more stuff to do in your busy life!

The great thing is that there really isn't a lot to learn. A friend beautifully described it as a spiral: the more you understand, the deeper it gets. Rather than at an intellectual, cognitive level, it's at an intuitive inner knowing level, like digesting slowly.

Can you think of a time when you had an inner knowing – it was a no-brainer, no decision was needed, you just 'knew'? What were the qualities about that moment? What was it like for you?

Often it seems so simple. I remember when I knew it was time to leave the finance industry and set up my own business. I realised it was the right thing to do. It just felt right. I didn't know exactly what I was going to do but that didn't matter; it would all be ok – and it has! This "knowing" seemed to come from my whole body rather than just my head.

Have you had that sense of 'inner knowing'? That's what we are looking for here. Not a cognitive understanding (well, that's a start!), a new deep inner knowing, even un-learning or un-thinking!

What will you discover?

In this book you will:

- Bust the myths of confidence
- Realise what confidence really means

- Learn what the Three Principles are
- Discover how this understanding changes everything
- See through the illusions of where our experience comes from
- Learn about the mechanics of our thinking
- Be aware of the costs of lack of confidence
- Reap the rewards from rediscovering your inner confidence

Throughout the book you will read real-life case studies from many of my clients. I am so grateful that they gave their permission to include these so that you can have your own insights. I have also included some of my own experience – both good and not so good. And of course, an explanation of these mysterious Three Principles that I keep talking about!

To get the best out of this book, I suggest you read this from a place of 'knowing nothing', a bit like a curious young child. Read it as if you are listening to your favourite piece of music; let the words float through you.

Please don't do any overthinking when you read this book – what lands, will land and you can always re-read (I have kept this book short on purpose). Just be easy with yourself – read a bit and then let what you have read sit with you. Then you will have insights of your own.

My aim is that by the end of this book you realise that confidence is a given, it is part of your blue print. You already have it – you just weren't aware of this. I will be focusing on confidence; however the by-product of this is that you will notice that you feel less stressed. With the energy that used to be consumed by overthinking, you will notice that you are more productive. Life will seem easier. And even if this doesn't happen straight away – just let things rest. It *will* happen, allow yourself time.

As Sydney Banks (an incredible man who's changed many people's lives enormously, whom I will introduce later in this book) says in The Missing Link:

> *In the loving voice of an author who speaks from the certainty of enlightenment, this book offers solace to the world-weary, hope to the discouraged, direction to the lost and contentment to the discontented.*

What wonderful words, and I hope that this book touches you in a similar way.

Chapter 3: Busting the Myths of Confidence

Pay no attention to what the critics say. A statue has never been erected in honour of a critic.

JEAN SIBELIUS

Chapter 3: Busting the Myths of Confidence

There are so many misunderstandings surrounding what confidence really means, that I think it is important to start by busting some myths. This simple word has caused confusion for so many people and furthermore, stopped many of them from being confident.

One client, Jenny, wanted to feel confident at work. I asked her what confidence meant to her, and she described the behaviour of some of her work colleagues who she believed as being confident. Let's just say that her descriptions weren't particularly flattering. Words such as arrogant, know-it-all and aggressive passed her lips. Those attributes were so against her values it was no wonder she wasn't confident!

Once Jenny appreciated what confidence really meant – she had a momentous lightbulb moment. I can still picture her beaming face and shoulders relaxing when she 'got it'.

Just like Jenny, many people have a false perception of what confidence means. The issue with this is that it affects how they behave – whether that means playing small or putting on an act to beef themselves up.

Before I share with you what confidence really means – let's have a look at some of the myths.

MYTH NUMBER ONE: Overconfidence

> **Definition of Overconfident** (Oxford Dictionary)
>
> *Excessively confident.*
>
> "Sarah's downfall came through being overconfident"
>
> *Synonyms*: cocksure, smug, conceited, self-assured, self-assertive, unabashed, brash, swaggering, blustering, overbearing, overweening, presuming, presumptuous, riding/heading for a fall, foolhardy.

Not very complimentary is it?

During the Confidence Workshops I run, we often explore the behaviours of overconfident people. Here are some of the descriptions that people have shared:

- Coming across as a 'know-it all'
- Enjoys putting other people down
- Having to always be right

- Adopting an overly commanding posture
- Talk *at* people rather than *with* people
- Invading others' personal space
- Being arrogant.

People who behave arrogantly seem as if they have all the confidence in the world; however this is often just a façade. They have as many underlying issues, vulnerabilities or fears, as people who are reserved and shy. They hide behind thick armour which they think protects them. Sadly they erroneously believe that behaving this way will make them feel good – an 'outside-in' delusion – which we will explore later.

I can relate to this – not my proudest of times. In my 20s, I behaved in a very arrogant way at work, especially during meetings. I believed that if I was aggressive I would get my own way, rather than listen and accept someone else's point of view. I shudder when I think about it. A few years later a colleague, who was much older than me, admitted that he used to be petrified of me, oh dear!

I thought that I would get people's respect, far from it. I noticed that people would avoid me and what's more, I didn't feel good about myself.

Do you recognise any of this within yourself?

You don't need to behave in an arrogant way and undermine others; all you are doing is undermining yourself. It may seem that this behaviour gives you power – it doesn't. If you want power, you are looking in the wrong place.

The term 'overconfident' is an oxymoron – you know deep down that you don't feel confident and hope that compensating for this will distract people from your vulnerabilities. Is that correct? Now let's bust the myth that 'overconfident' people are confident...

You may not recognise 'overconfidence' in yourself and moreover, you may feel intimidated by overconfident people. Perhaps it seems as if these people make you lose confidence and leave you feeling small, insecure and even scared?

Later in this book, we are going to learn that all of our feelings come from our thoughts in the moment. We experience the world not from the outside (yes – I know it seems that way – just bear with me) but from our thinking. So 'intimidated' thinking will cause you to feel intimidated!

Imagine seeing these overconfident people with compassion; seeing beyond their arrogant behaviour and realising that this is just a smoke screen to hide their vulnerabilities. Perhaps you can experience them in a very different light now?

When you have security within yourself, you won't feel threatened. Actually, you will find that you have the inner strength to behave however your wisdom guides you; whether that means removing yourself from the situation, saying something assertively in a compassionate way, or just doing nothing. Myth busted! Got it?

MYTH NUMBER TWO: "I was born shy!"

Our next myth is that you need to be an extrovert to be confident.

> **Definition of Extrovert** (Oxford Dictionary)
>
> *An outgoing, socially confident person.*
>
> "Like most extroverts he was a good dancer"
>
> *Synonyms:* outgoing person, sociable person, life and soul of the party, socialiser, mixer, mingler, social butterfly, socialite party animal.

Good grief, even the definition suggests that

extroverts are confident! What a huge generalisation.

Shyness can be debilitating, affecting your social and work life. You may prefer to avoid certain situations and hide in your shell (can you see how similar this is to overconfident people wearing their metaphoric thick armour?).

Does the thought of attending social gatherings bring on panic attacks? Do you get the cold sweats at the thought of being with so many people and having to think of things to say? The mindless small talk might send you running or leave you tongue-tied. Even if it's not that bad – you may experience times when you end up doubting yourself as that old inner critic whirs into action.

I used to internally hear "Lindsey, keep your mouth shut, you are thick as two short planks!" on a regular basis. This was not exactly helpful when I was trying to raise enough confidence to talk with people.

Some of us don't have a critical inner dialogue; maybe instead your mind simply goes blank as the brain's instinctive 'fight, flight or freeze' response kicks in.

Many clients have shared with me that they have 'always' been shy and I usually reply; "You weren't born shy though". They agree, however for some, they can't remember life any other way.

So let's have a look at where all this shyness may have stemmed from…

Professor Jerome Kagan, Professor of Psychology at Harvard University and one of the key pioneers of developmental psychology, conducted a study in 1994 on child behaviour. He studied children from four months old until seven years old and noticed the difference in their reactions to unfamiliar situations.

Some children were highly sensitive to unexpected or unfamiliar events and would kick their legs and feet more, cry longer and louder. They had higher heart rates and their limbic system that controlled their emotions was more easily aroused - a significant biological difference when compared to the children who were more comfortable in these situations.

This type of behaviour, being sensitive to sudden change or highly stimulating environments, was consistent in these children over the whole period of time they were studied.

So imagine a young boy who has an Aunt that he doesn't see often. When she comes to visit, she goes up close, pinches his cheeks fondly and talks loudly at him. What do you think he will do? Most likely he will hide behind his Mum, wanting to avoid this stranger. And what might his Mum say, "Oh don't mind him – he's shy".

Without the mother being aware, this type of name calling then develops into a belief for the child. As he got older, he was much happier being on his own; he felt content. At school, he may have been called anti-social or a loner. If only people would realise the impact of name-calling!

When I shared this scenario with a client, he said that this sounded just like his own experience.

He found being with people exhausting. He much preferred being on his own and would feel more energised then. He believed that he was shy, not good with people and generally anti-social, all of which affected his confidence levels. He would get anxious if he knew that he had to socialise! He believed his shy thoughts and allowed them to make him feel shy.

We are all different – unique. This client didn't need

fixing; he didn't need to learn confidence techniques. Once he understood the mechanics of his thinking and accepted himself, that he preferred having alone time and that this was fine, his anxieties and stress gradually just evaporated.

As Bernardo J. Carducci, Director of the Shyness Research Institute, Indiana writes:

> *The notion that people are born shy is simply a belief about shyness, not a fact... biology is not destiny.*

Our feelings and experience comes from our thoughts. The identity of being shy stems from thought. If we keep thinking that we are shy and we do this hundreds of times over – then of course we are going to feel shy. Is that a wise move? Forget the identities that have been given to you in the past, whether by others or even by yourself. You are so much more than them.

Later in this book I will share in greater depth the incredible power of understanding how we really work as human beings, such as we are thinkers, but we are not thoughts! You don't need to get caught up in the illusion of your thinking. When that happens, these old, outdated identities that you have been labelled just drop off – into the bin.

You were not born shy. Confidence is not based on whether you are an extrovert or introvert. You may prefer to have time on your own or would rather spend it with people - both are fine. You don't need these labels or identities; you are highly adaptive, the neuroplasticity of your brain continuously evolves throughout your life, so you change whether you realise it or not.

Confidence has nothing to do with how well you get on with people either. Another myth busted! Got it?

MYTH NUMBER THREE: Competent

> **Definition of Competent** (Oxford Dictionary)
>
> *Having the necessary ability, knowledge, or skill to do something successfully.*
>
> "A highly competent surgeon"
>
> *Synonyms:* acquainted with, familiar with, with knowledge of, with an understanding of, conversant with, au courant with, au fait with.

Please note that this definition has nothing to do with confidence. So why is it here? The reason is because I have heard many people misinterpret competence for confidence.

You can be competent and not feel confident. You can be competent and feel confident. You can not be competent and not feel confident, and you can not be competent and feel confident. Phew!

One client, Lily, believed that people were confident if they were able to stand and speak in public. At business network meetings she would judge her own public speaking ability against others. Her inner chatter of not feeling good enough compared with others knocked her confidence. What she was doing was getting confidence muddled up with competence; public speaking is merely a skill, which can be learnt.

We often read that famous comedians or actors who seem so confident in the public eye actually suffer from low self-esteem and lack of confidence. The late David Bowie, legendary English singer, songwriter and actor, told Q magazine that in the heyday of the early 70s:

I had enormous self-image problems and very low self-esteem, which I hid behind obsessive writing and performing. I was driven to get through life very quickly, I really felt so utterly inadequate. I thought the work was the only thing of value.

Both David Bowie and my client Lily determined that their low self-esteem came from comparing and judging themselves and others. In reality, their thoughts and consequent feelings of inadequacy were what actually caused their suffering.

When we have less noise in our heads and our thoughts are less busy, busy, busy; when we have clearer minds and we are calm, quiet, peaceful, it is amazing how we can effortlessly improve and thrive in the moment.

I used to believe that I couldn't write. It would take me sometimes a whole morning just to write 500 words. Now, I am so enjoying writing this book, the words just seem to flow from me effortlessly.

Even though confidence doesn't mean competence – it is incredible how our skills can easily improve!

I hope that these myths about confidence have been busted and that you have got it! Now, it is about time that I share with you what confidence really means.

Chapter 4: Confidence – What is it?

It's me who is my enemy
Me who beats me up
Me who makes the monsters
Me who strips my confidence.
PAULA COLE, *'Me' in the Album 'This Fire'*

Chapter 4: Confidence – What is it?

So if confidence is not about being overly confident or competent - what is it?

> **Definition of Confidence** (Oxford Dictionary)
>
> *A feeling or belief that one can have faith in or rely on someone or something.*
>
> *A feeling of self-assurance arising from an appreciation of one's own abilities or qualities.*

When researching confidence many years ago, I discovered that the origin of the word comes from Latin *"confidentia"* from the verb *confidere*, which means, "**to have full trust**".

Please stop and read that again: **"to have full trust"**.

If you had full trust in yourself, what would be different for you?

True confidence is all about trusting yourself – no matter what is happening on the outside - and having absolute trust that you are okay and you can get through the richness that life has to offer, both the challenging and rewarding.

I remember at the end of 1992 our Queen Elizabeth II

described the year as *"annus horribilis"*. Her eldest son, Prince Charles separated from Princess Diana; her daughter the Princess Royal divorced; the tabloids had a field day with photos of the Queen's daughter-in-law Sarah Ferguson topless and Windsor Castle almost burned down. Despite all that, the Queen got through it.

In late 2011 to 2012, I had a personal *"annus horribilis"*. My Dad died within 24 hours of getting pneumonia, my Mum was having violent episodes while suffering with dementia, three other family members passed away (one of which was a suicide), my father-in-law got cancer and to cap it all off, my husband suddenly lost his job. I remember sitting in my office taking a deep breath and sensing that we would get through that year, older and wiser.

I feel very fortunate that I had studied and rediscovered my inner confidence, giving me the resilience to face it all head on. That was even before I discovered the life-changing approach that I will be sharing with you in this book! We all have the capacity of innate wellbeing and confidence. It is the nature of who we are; even though we often don't realise this, it is still true.

A lovely young man Harold, a psychology student, attended one of my Confidence Workshops as he wanted to experience what I was teaching, so came as my guest. When I shared the meaning of the word confidence, he got so excited. Afterwards he said:

> *I learned to have full trust in myself. Once I grasped that concept, I saw things in a different light. I can honestly say that I could have left the workshop within the first 15 minutes and come out saying that it was absolutely worth it.*

What a wonderful insight. By having full trust in ourselves, inner confidence is a given, and we can then accept ourselves, warts and all!

Nobody lacks confidence

"What?" you may be asking. You may think that you are lacking confidence, but you are not. Confidence is part of us – it is in the nature of being human. You and I were both born with confidence. Everyone is. You don't lack confidence – you just obscure it. You conceal it with insecure, fearful feelings and thoughts. Without those, confidence is a given. Lacking confidence does not exist. Got it?

Now, let's explore what these Three Principles are...

Chapter 5: An Introduction to Three Principles

Someone once said to me, "Are you telling me that chair isn't real, that it's only thought?" I said, "Of course the chair is real. But it comes to you via thought."

SYDNEY BANKS

Chapter 5: An Introduction to Three Principles

Now that you know that confidence means: 'to have full inner trust', you may be wondering how you get that inner trust.

As mentioned in the second chapter, this book is not a 'how to'. There are no step-by-step guides. I remember when I first discovered what I am sharing with you I thought, "how do I do this? What are the steps?" We are so conditioned to want the step-by-step guides. I used to offer clients the 'how to' and 'step-by-step guide' (and for any of my previous clients reading this book, here is a huge apology!). I was doing my best with the knowledge that I had at the time. My intentions were well meaning.

Reading the many books on confidence on my bookshelf – the chapters include:

- How to overcome fear
- How to change your beliefs
- How to have positive self-talk
- How to get confidence from others
- How to change the movies in your mind
- How to say "no"
- How to look the part

'How to' gives you more things to think about and what I have now grasped is that *this* is half of the problem. I'm sure you already have enough on your mind, without anything more.

So what am I directing you towards?

I mentioned in Chapter one that I had won a free place on a workshop. This was called "He'Art of Thriving" run by Kimberley Hare. I originally met Kim in 2007 on one of her Train the Trainer courses. In recent years I noticed that her blogs had changed and was intrigued as to why.

Before going on the workshop, Kimberley suggested that I read some books based on something called the Three Principles. So I diligently read not one, but quite a few – and I haven't stopped since!

The Three Principles are principles about *being human*. It's not about how to, techniques, analysis, modelling or the X steps. It is about understanding how and that we experience the world. When we appreciate and comprehend these principles there really is nothing to do. They allow us to realise that we already have all the answers to our own questions somewhere within.

The Three Principles are:

Mind: The source of all intelligence. We exist, we are made of energy and our existence and energy is universal

Consciousness: Allows us to be aware of our existence

Thought: Guides us through life as free-thinkers. We bring our consciousness alive through our thinking.

These are basic building blocks to understanding ourselves as humans and our mental behaviour. They create all of our human experience; mental functionality cannot exist without these. As these are principles – they are descriptive rather than prescriptive. They are solid and the basic fundamental nature of us as humans.

What I am talking about here is not a philosophy, religion or psychological theory. It is simply a principle with three components to it. Ultimately the Three Principles are one 'conscious thinking mind'. It's true about us even when we don't know this. When we connect with this at a deep level – well, for me it is like coming home, coming back to my roots as a human being.

Now, you may be thinking that you need to do something. I know, that is what I thought when I first came across the Three Principles. However as I am sharing with you a description then the only thing you need to do is to see and experience this for yourself. That's it!

You don't need to change your thinking from negative to positive (thoughts are neutral – more on that later). You don't need to stop thinking (you are human, we all think, it would be unnatural if you stopped thinking and life would be very boring!).

Please just let the words wash over you, read this like it is a piece of music as I suggested in the first chapter. Perhaps there are elements that connect with you instantly, snippets of music that resonate or perhaps there is something about the whole sound that feels right – or not! Either way, that's ok. When we listen to music without overthinking or trying to interpret it – it just flows.

I am so excited about sharing this with you! I love simplicity and these principles are so simple yet so deep. They are relevant to every person on our planet. You, me, your family, friends, neighbours, strangers… every single one!

Remember, this book has no techniques, steps or the need to model others. We already have the innate wisdom, mental and emotional health and confidence within us, we were born that way.

Understanding the Three Principles have helped:

- People who suffered from anxiety or depression. They now live with ease and joy in their world
- Business owners and leaders who were stressed, inefficient and feeling a failure feel more fulfilled and overcome issues with vigour and creativity
- Struggling relationships where there was confusion, upsets and unhappiness. They are now enjoying more love, respect and closeness than they ever thought possible; either together or apart
- Children in and out of schools, where problems of bullying, self-harming, truancy and drug problems have been eliminated and where performance and enjoyment of learning has improved
- People who had addictions, they realise that they don't need to live in their compulsive

world. They become free of their cravings and lead healthy and happy lives

- People trying to cope with life threatening illnesses which were overtaking their lives are able to live more peacefully even when facing death
- Convicts have found freedom for the first time in their lives, even when confined to prison, and have been able to move forward with hope and forgiveness of their past.

In the next chapter I introduce you to Sydney Banks who, through having an enlightened experience, discovered and subsequently shared the foundation of all human experience. These have existed and been referred to many times for thousands of years. Yet Sydney explained this basic truth in such a simple, yet effective way – changing the course of psychology. Then I will explain the Three Principles at a deeper level.

Chapter 6: Who was Sydney Banks?

From a state of not knowing you are likely to see something new.

SYDNEY BANKS

Chapter 6: Who was Sydney Banks?

Sydney Banks was an extraordinary and humble man. You may not have heard of him as he kept away from the media, however by sharing his insights in such a simple way, he has changed and transformed thousands, if not millions of lives... including my own, my clients' and now hopefully yours.

He died in May 2009 and his teaching is still being passed on - which is exactly what I aim to do in this book.

Syd came from very humble beginnings. He was born in Scotland and was adopted as a baby, growing up with his new family. He moved to Canada and became a welder by trade.

His insights started when he and his wife, Barb, went to an 'awareness group' weekend (the 'in' thing in the early 1970s). They got chatting to a young couple and shared their worries and insecurities with one another. As they were leaving the workshop Syd bumped into the young man again, who was a psychologist. This young man said to Syd, "You know Syd – you told me you were insecure and I've never heard such nonsense in all my life". This had a profound effect on Syd:

> *What I heard was: there's no such thing as insecurity, it's only thought. All my insecurity was only my own thoughts! It was like a bomb going off in my head... It was so enlightening! It was unbelievable. [And after that] there was such beauty coming into my life.*
> SYDNEY BANKS *'The Truth Lies Within,' Part 2 of the 'Long Beach Lecture Series'*

A few days later Syd could hear his wife and mother-in-law complaining about the change in him and how happy he suddenly was. Apparently he burst out laughing, annoying his mother-in-law even further. He knew he needed to say something and just as he was going to open his mouth, he had an amazing, enlightening experience.

I watched a video of Syd talking about this moment and also in his Long Beach tapes he shared that what he encountered was beyond near death experience.

He *went through to the other side of death and that there is nothing to fear.* He lost all sense of self; entering and being surrounded by shimmering white light. He had a deep and intense feeling of peace, calm, love and transformational awareness that all of life is pure, formless energy.

In Elsie Spittle's book *Beyond Imagination*, she shares that:

> *After his enlightenment, his whole persona changed to one of confidence; his presence was imbued with an energy I'd never seen in him before. He told us he had discovered the secret to life; that the Three Principles he had uncovered had the power to change the fields of psychology and psychiatry forever. He said these Principles would help alleviate humanity's suffering like nothing before.*

Ten months after this realisation, Syd gave up his job as a welder and began sharing his insights and wisdom with thousands of people. He spoke at Universities to psychology students, in prisons to inmates, to people all over the English-speaking world.

Here was a man who had only a basic education; however he had changed and gained such wisdom which he then shared, impacting millions of people's lives.

Sydney Banks described the Three Principles as:

Mind, which is the source of all intelligence, Consciousness, which allows us to be aware of our existence, and Thought, which guides us through the world we live in as free-thinking agents.

The key to understanding human behaviour. They are the "missing link" humanity has been searching for throughout history.

So let's begin to explore these Three Principles in more depth...

Chapter 7: Let's go Deeper!

I am satisfied with the mystery of life's eternity and with a knowledge, a sense, of the marvellous structure of existence — as well as the humble attempt to understand even a tiny portion of the Reason that manifests itself in nature.
ALBERT EINSTEIN *Mein Weltbild (My World-view) (1931)*

Chapter 7: Let's go Deeper!

Principle of Mind:

Beyond our cognitive thinking, we already have such amazing wisdom. Our **mind,** or you could call this universal energy, innate intelligence, intuition, your soul, is all formless. Mind is not purely the brain – we are so much more than this – mind is even bigger than self.

We are made from universal matter and energy. Without energy we wouldn't exist, it is our life force. It is the source of everything in the universe and we are part of that. This is huge! It's limitless and ever-present. You cannot destroy energy – it simply transforms.

I hope you can begin to appreciate that you are far more than your anxieties, worries and issues. When you are not tied up in your thinking, things always work out okay. You have innate mental well-being, limitless creativity and wisdom.

Can you recall any experiences when you suddenly had a lightbulb moment and insight just popped up from nowhere? A problem that you have ruminated with the previous day is resolved suddenly in a moment. Do you find that when you stop thinking about a problem then the solution often appears? You cannot remember a person's name and then as soon as you stop thinking about it, you've got it!

I often get my best ideas when I am doing mindless tasks such as hanging out the washing or having a shower. So how is it that these insights don't come when we badly need them - when we are stressed and busy? Usually we are so caught up in our thinking that the insights cannot find a way through the whirring thoughts in our heads.

I believe that Einstein understood this fully and capitalised in this knowledge. He loved spending time relaxing and going for long walks. I read somewhere that he would have a nap in the afternoon and hold a pen. When he dropped the pen, the noise would wake him and he would write down the first thought that came through his mind.

Isn't it interesting that he had loads of insights and ideas? He described his insight of the Theory of General Relativity as "the happiest thought of my life".

I believe in intuition and inspiration... At times I feel certain I am right while not knowing the reason.

ALBERT EINSTEIN

These insights and inspirations all support the Principle that you have universal intelligence. When you get out of your own way, then the answer will pop up without you needing to do anything. So what is the point of worrying or getting stuck in your problems? That's not where the answers lie.

The answers come from your innate mind, inbuilt confidence, intelligence, intuition, formless energy, or whatever you want to call it. When you take off the pressure, the rush and urgency, and give yourself some space, things seem to flow naturally. It may sound counter-intuitive but we know it works.

We are conditioned to believe that we need to constantly analyse and review. Yet all we are doing then is recalling, rather than allowing ourselves to have fresh thinking! If you have an issue, just write it down and leave it. (in fact you don't really need to do that!) Trust and allow your own wisdom the space to operate naturally without disturbance.

We are amazing. Our bodies and minds have the capacity to self-correct and heal, like a roly-poly Weeble doll. Because of the self-correcting nature of your mind, it means that you can leave it be, not obscure your mind with worry or conflict. Then you will innately get back to neutral and a state of well-being.

Our family were coming to stay over Christmas so I cleaned the house from top to bottom (a rare occurrence). Whilst dusting, I got a massive splinter in my finger. I thought I had removed it all, however the area became red and sore. I kept fiddling with it, poking it, scraping it and it continued to hurt. The redness wasn't spreading so I knew that it wasn't infected. My husband told me to just leave it alone and that if anything was still in there my body would naturally get rid of it. I eventually left it alone. Twenty eight days later the splinter literally flew out of my finger! My body had naturally self-healed when I left it alone to do its magic. Isn't that amazing?

When you slow down and give yourself some space, your innate wisdom and mind has the capacity to give you answers easily and effortlessly. Insights will show up more often.

Have you ever played the Yellow Car game during a

long journey? (You get a point every time you spot a yellow car, calling it out before your fellow passengers). Insights are a bit like yellow cars. Once you start looking for them, it's amazing how many you begin to see!

You already have a built-in operating solution and self-healing system that works. Let it, allow it, and trust it to work! You will save yourself so much time and reduce your stress level. Hence you already have the answers to a confident, productive and stress-free life.

Got it?

Principle of Consciousness:

Our **consciousness** brings to life our thoughts, making them rich with colour, detail, feelings, sounds, smells and taste. So it's our thoughts, together with consciousness, that create our reality. Both make our experiences seem real. This is true for every human being – hence it is a principle. Essentially, there would be no reality without consciousness and thought. We wouldn't know we even existed!

I have heard a few times an analogy of a projector

that brings what I am sharing with you to life:

In order for the projector (consciousness) to work, it needs a source of energy (mind). The images on the screen (thoughts) won't be seen without the projector. And of course, even though the images can seem so real, they are not.

How often do we get really emotional when watching a film even though we know that it is all made up, with actors and sometimes computer generated scenes? And there we are, blubbering even though we know that the film isn't real.

The screen is like the outside world; the screen is the same, however it depends on the quality of the projector and resolution and clarity of the film as to the quality which projects *onto* the screen.

I read a great quote from the website of *Insight Principles*:

> *Blaming the external world for our experience is like blaming our shadow for being overweight. A shadow is merely a reflection. It has no existence independent of the light and the object the light is shining upon.*

Our moods go up and down and when we have insight that this is natural and that they rise and fall, then we don't need to be concerned about them. If you feel low, nervous, unconfident, happy, and ecstatic, all of these are fine. You can feel comfortable with any of these emotions. None is 'bad'. You don't need to struggle to change these types of moods. In fact, you will find that your state of mind changes naturally anyway when you leave it alone. Our moods are completely made up, coming from our thinking.

Our inbuilt equaliser

Recently I was asked to be interviewed for an online broadcast lecture on Body Language. I was quite relaxed about this until the day of the broadcast. A family member asked me what preparation I had done. Hmm... not much! I had run workshops on this subject in the past so had felt comfortable about the subject matter. And then I started to feel a tingle in my stomach. It grew and grew until a tight knot metaphorically formed. "What if I can't answer the questions?" "What if I sound stupid?" My nerves were getting the better of me. I quickly researched about body language on the internet. There was so much information that I felt momentarily overwhelmed.

Underneath all this concern I knew deep down that I would be ok. It was merely noise, like a howling storm, and I knew it would pass.

I left in plenty of time and five miles into the journey found myself in a traffic jam. I sat stationary, the clock ticking and the satnav showing that I was going to arrive ten minutes late. Luckily I had saved the interviewer's phone number so informed him of the situation. By the time I had arrived – even later as I couldn't find the place – my level of mood had sunk even further. And yet again, I knew I'd be ok. Perhaps it wouldn't be one of my best talks, but I'd be good enough.

I got into the room and I could see the concern on the faces of the organisers as there was something wrong with the sound quality. There was no more that I could do. I knew that it was nothing but my own thinking causing me to feel anxious. It wasn't the interview or how much research I had or hadn't done. It was my level of consciousness based on my own thoughts I was getting caught up in. Seeing through this illusion, I relaxed in the moment and the level of my well-being rose.

When I reflected on this episode it was as if my moods were being adjusted similar to an equaliser on a music amp; at times the control was turned low and in a moment turned high. An equaliser's job is to strengthen or weaken the level of a specific frequency range. My consciousness is like my very own inbuilt equaliser!

Once we appreciate that it is natural for us to have various levels of moods, our inherent system has the capacity to take us back to being in balance. We don't need to manage or control our thinking, our moods. Knowing this makes a huge difference to the quality of our well-being.

Our experience comes from our mind, consciousness and thought 100% of the time.

It's the level of this that defines the quality of our experience. For example, if our mood is low and insecure, then our 'reality' of life will be low, with insecure and anxious feelings. If our mood is high, then life seems wonderful, easy and calm.

Consciousness is what brings our thoughts and our senses to light, creating our experience of life. Rather than getting involved in the content of our personal experience, at a deeper level we can see behind the scenes and value where our human experience is evolved from. I have noticed in myself that I am disassociated to the content and noise of thought and more associated in the beauty of life in the moment.

Principle of Thought:

We all have thoughts each and every moment of the day. Isn't that wonderful? Our thinking gives us our experience of life. We are thinkers. We have many thoughts; however *we are not our thoughts.* It is our thoughts that enable us to experience, to acknowledge and respond to life, that is all, *finito.*

How many?

How many thoughts do we, on average, have in a day? When I have asked clients this in the past I have heard anything from 5,000 to one million (there are some very busy minds out there).

The LONI (Laboratory Of Neuro Imaging) at University of Southern California did some preliminary studies with student volunteers and estimated that we have around 60-70,000 thoughts per day. They also found that there is no generally accepted definition of what 'thought' is or how it is created. In their study, they assumed that

> ...a 'thought' is a sporadic single-idea cognitive
> concept resulting from the act of thinking, or
> produced by spontaneous systems-level cognitive
> brain activations.

Before I found the above study, I estimated that we have about one thought a second. As there are 86,400 seconds in a twenty four hour period (we still have thoughts in our dreams when we are asleep), perhaps my estimate was a little bit high. However I have known many people who overthink constantly – actually, I used to. My brain never stopped! Our thoughts can wander; in one moment, we can move through one thought to another…

I have just stopped writing and looked out at the window and saw a robin still in flight, peck a blackberry from our bush. What an amazing sight. How lucky that I stopped typing in that very moment! Robins are such beautiful, friendly birds and for some reason they always remind me of my Nan.

And now I can hear an ice cream van playing its tune and remember a friend sharing with me that her parents told her that if the ice cream van had music playing, it meant that it had run out of ice cream… and all those interlinked thoughts happened within a couple of seconds.

Even in the time that I have typed those here, my wave of thoughts have continued on, rolling through my mind, passing by just as quickly as they arrived.

Our thoughts are brainwaves and many of these we take no notice of. They just float by.

The illusion

Often it seems as if the outside world 'makes' us think a certain way. Watching details of war on the news 'makes' us feel sad, sunny days 'make' us feel happy, certain relationships 'make' us frustrated, losing our job 'makes' us lose confidence, a holiday 'makes' us rest…

Sorry folks, this is all an illusion. It's not the outside that 'makes' us do or be anything. It is actually our thinking that creates our experience and our feelings of sad, happy, frustrated, unconfident, rested... Our feelings are simply coming from our thoughts in the moment.

Yes, I know it seems as if our emotions and experiences come from the outside world. That's what I used to believe, however, do you react in the same way all the time? Aren't we more flexible than that? Can you remember times when a situation or person didn't annoy you, whereas other times when it (or they) did?

Our youngest son was back from University so occasionally I'd take a morning cup of tea to him. As I walked into his bedroom I was greeted with clutter, clothes thrown on the floor (a 'floordrobe' according to him). Now and then I felt really frustrated but would manage to hold my tongue, other times I'd bark at him to clear the mess up, and then sometimes it just didn't bother me at all. The room was always the same – cluttered and messy*. The difference was my thoughts.

The point of this example isn't about the messy room – it is that my reaction comes from my thoughts. Sometimes I remember this, sometimes I don't. In either case, it is still my own thinking creating my experience in the moment, just as it is for you.

*FYI I waited until I was in a calm state of mind to have a conversation with my son about his room; shouting would only antagonise us. And I have noticed an improvement!

It seems that the outside creates our experience. It's like an illusion: sometimes we create fantastic illusions, other times horrible ones.

Your thoughts are like the artist's brush. They create a personal picture of the reality you live in.
SYDNEY BANKS

Our whole experience all of the time comes from our own thoughts. I remember when I first realised this, I understood it at a cognitive level...however when I really understood this, an inner knowing, it has changed everything as I have shared earlier in this book.

When I share this with others, sometimes they say that a trigger causes them to have an intense strong feeling instantly. It seems as though they didn't have any thoughts. It happens so quickly is there any time for a thought to enter their mind, be processed and have such an effect? Yes! They must have had a thought for that emotion or feeling to arise. We always feel our thoughts, even when we don't realise it.

As a human, you have a very useful inbuilt system (via feelings and emotions) that is your compass, indicating the state of your thinking. Allow this inbuilt system to guide you back to a calm mind!

The Principle of Thought directs us to appreciate that:

- 100% of our experience is created by our thoughts from the inside-out
- We are always feeling our thoughts
- We can have new thought at any time.

...Got it?

Chapter 8: You are an Amazing Magician

There are only two ways to live your life. One is as though nothing is a miracle. The other is as though everything is a miracle.

Attributed to ALBERT EINSTEIN *as quoted in Journal of France and Germany (1942–1944) by Gilbert Fowler White*

Chapter 8: You are an Amazing Magician

Have you ever seen a magic trick and then found out how it was done? With that new knowledge, you will never be able to watch that trick again and be fooled. Now it seems so obvious that you can't believe how others cannot see through the illusion!

I remember seeing a short video on Facebook where a playing card was shown, the 'magician' swiped it down and hey presto it turned into a bank note. Magic!

He then showed how it was done. The card had a crease in the middle, so when he stroked it, it easily doubled over revealing the bank note, which was stuck on the back of the card. Easy when you know how! When you see the truth, that's it, you can't go back to not knowing.

Since then I have made a similar card with a £20 note and occasionally demonstrate the trick to my clients (a few of them have told me not to give up the day job – my magic skills clearly need a bit of work!).

That's how it is with our experience. It seems that the outside 'makes' us feel a certain way. However when we see through the illusion, that our experience is based on our thinking and feelings and brought to life via consciousness – it changes everything. And we don't need to do anything! Afterwards our life is the same, however everything seems so different. It's as if we've taken off a pair of murky glasses and can now see clearly; we are no longer fooled by the illusion.

> *One Mind. One Consciousness. One Thought. If any one of those disappear there is no reality. You must have a Thought to take Consciousness and turn it into life for you. And there can't be Consciousness without Universal Intelligence, Mind, creating Consciousness.*
> SYDNEY BANKS

We notice our thoughts and feelings and then for some bizarre reason we put judgements on them. "That's a negative thought – I must change this to a positive one." I used to get trapped in that way of thinking; I even used to point this out to clients.

Remember: a thought is just a thought, which is a thought...

The key is to recognise that we have many thoughts in a day, so it's important not to get caught up in them or take all of them seriously.

For example, recently I was in a traffic jam (a different one from the previous chapter!), yet there was hardly any traffic coming the other way. For a moment the thought of overtaking on the wrong side of the road popped into my head. I would get to the roundabout so much quicker! I imagined the other drivers sitting open mouthed at me overtaking them so dangerously. These thoughts came into my mind, but do you think I acted on them? No, of course not! We have all these thoughts that travel through our minds, some helpful, some less so. We don't need to act on or believe all of them.

Some days, the mind can imagine a whole load of garbage, but our thoughts can also be amazing!

As I sit and write this there is music playing on the radio... The intricacy of the sounds, the arrangement of the orchestra, the singers, the conductor, the band, all working together to form such a beautiful sound. Suddenly I am absorbed by it, whilst just a moment ago I was oblivious to it. And where did this originate? Thought.

The capacity of thought is huge. Infinite. Look around you – what can you see? Cars? Houses? All the items in your home? The book you are reading? All of these are created from thought. Our thoughts have the potential to transform the formless into form. Wow!

We have the ability to have fresh thinking in every moment. The gift of thought is incredible. It's a bit like fire. Fire has the capacity to warm our homes or to move a huge steam train, as well as the power to burn acres of land and destroy habitats.

One thought has the capacity to change a person in any moment.

Many years ago I really hated someone (no, I'm not proud of this). Every time they opened their mouth I felt annoyed. My face and body would automatically tense up. I believed that their critical comments made me feel unconfident.

This person was coming to stay with us…for quite some time. How on earth was I going to cope?

When they arrived, I took them to their bedroom and we got talking. I was being polite and so listened to them, gritting my teeth. I noticed that they were opening up and sharing their story. I stopped and listened, really listened, and finally heard them. I saw life through their eyes. And in a split second I went from a place of hate to love. One thought in the moment changed my perception of them in a flash. Our relationship instantly changed from hate to love, and I have loved that person dearly ever since.

The great thing is that by noticing your thoughts through consciousness, you can use this inbuilt 'tool' of thinking if you want to. Any thoughts that don't serve you, you can just let these go... Rest assured that the next thought is queuing up, eager to pop into your head the moment there is space!

> ### Mind + Consciousness + Thought = Magic

We all have mind, consciousness and thought. These three create our own magic allows us to see that confidence is a given. You don't lack confidence – it is always there – it is just obscured by insecure thinking.

If you wear a pair of dirty, smeary glasses then you cannot see the world clearly. And if you have insecure, anxious, doubting thinking, you cannot see your own confidence within. You are hiding it.

Confidence is part of your blueprint therefore there is no absence, lack or flaw – it gets hidden,

concealed by insecure thinking.

On one of my Confidence Workshops, I asked clients to write down what they felt makes them lack confidence. When we explored the 30+ reasons – the root of every single one of them stemmed from... you've guessed it: **thought**, which **consciousness** brings to life, created by universal **mind**.

> *There is no end or limitations, nor are there boundaries to the human mind.*
> SYDNEY BANKS

And so thank you to Sydney Banks, an ordinary – extra-ordinary person, just like you and me. However he had amazing insights. These are not some fluffy theory; these are principles that are true for all humans.

Chapter 9: Brain Waves and Ocean Waves

I am not afraid of storms for I am learning how to sail my ship.

LOUISA MAY ALCOTT

Chapter 9: Brain Waves and Ocean Waves

We have learnt that we all have thousands of thoughts a day, as well as the capacity of our thoughts and the realisation that we don't need to get caught up in them. (Remember: we are thinkers, we are not our thoughts!)

But what are thoughts?

Ok – here's the science bit. When we have a thought, an electrical nerve impulse travels along an axon and triggers the nerve ending of a neuron to release a neurotransmitter. This builds a bridge across the synapse (gap) so it can bind with a receptor molecule like a key in a lock. This in turn converts the neurotransmitter back into an electrical nerve impulse. Each time this electrical charge is triggered, the synapses grow closer together. This then decreases the distance the electrical charge has to cross. Makes sense? Or should I say, got it?

Our brain is hypo-plastic – it adapts – therefore our thoughts reshape our brain.

If you have a thought which you *perceive* as negative and which causes you stress, then your brain fires off synapses of 'stress'. If this is done repeatedly, the stress hormone cortisol is released. This can adversely affect your immune system, your blood pressure goes up and your cholesterol rises. Your body tenses up, causing muscle tension and pain, you keep thinking these thoughts over and over and then you cannot sleep. The consequences of those negatively perceived thoughts? You could end up with a whole range of unpleasant physical and mental illnesses.

That's all rather gloomy! All from simply judging your own initial neutral thoughts as negative; forgetting that while we are thinkers, we are not our thoughts. Nor do we need to be!

Please take a second to read that again...**we are NOT our thoughts.** I'm going to keep repeating it throughout this book. The more people appreciate this, the better. The world will become a much calmer and content place – and we certainly need this!

What about the flip side? How would life be if you were able to effortlessly disregard all those thoughts that aren't helpful for you?

Meditation Research

Neuroscientist Sara Lazar had dreams of running the Boston Marathon but damaged her knee and back during early training. She came across a yoga class that promised to be vigorous and promoted flexibility, strength and cardio-vascular fitness. Sara decided to join the class, thinking that this would be a great way to keep fit and perhaps she would still be able to run the marathon.

During the classes, she became increasingly frustrated by the claims of the yoga teacher that she would feel calmer, have more compassion and become more open hearted. "Yeah, right!" Sara thought sarcastically. However, over the coming weeks all those claims did actually prove true. Sara noticed that she was able to deal with difficult situations more easily, without trying.

Being a scientist, she was curious. Was this just a placebo effect? She decided to do her own research into meditation, to determine whether it had any real effects on the brain.

To begin her research, Sara found 16 participants who had never done any meditation. They all completed a pre-questionnaire and their brains were scanned using an MRI machine (there was also a control group of non-meditators who had MRI brain scans as well).

The participants then went on an eight week Mindfulness-Based Stress Reduction (MBSR) Program at the University of Massachusetts Center for Mindfulness, and spent an average of twenty seven minutes each day practising the mindfulness exercises they were taught. After the eight weeks, they completed a post-questionnaire as well as having their brains MRI scanned once again.

The analysis of the MRI scans showed:

- An increase in grey-matter in the hippocampus – the area of the brain responsible for learning and memory
- Other areas changed relating to compassion, self-related processing and autobiographical memory
- A decrease in grey-matter in the amygdala – correlating to a reduction of stress levels as found in the post-questionnaires.

Although the practice of meditation is associated with a sense of peacefulness and physical relaxation, practitioners have long claimed that meditation also provides cognitive and psychological benefits that persist throughout the day. This study demonstrates that changes in brain

> *structure may underlie some of these reported improvements and that people are not just feeling better because they are spending time relaxing.*
> SARA LAZAR *PhD.*

Of course, this study focused on people 'doing' meditation. However the Three Principles show us that thought is merely a formless function, and you don't need to get caught up in it. You are a thinker, not your thoughts.

Not that there is anything wrong with practising meditation. What I am saying here is that by understanding the Three Principles, we enjoy the same benefits as 'doing' meditation without needing to 'do' anything. This would have saved the participants of the study over twenty five hours in those eight weeks!

Waves of Thought

For me, our thoughts are like waves in the ocean. Each moment there is a new wave, then another and another... continuously.

Sometimes, like life, the waves are strong; the force of the wind creating friction and great crescendos of water crashing with immense power. Between each crash there are moments of silence, broken quickly by the next forceful impact.

At other times the waves are gentle, caressing the sea with bubbling froth; calm, allowing the sediment to settle, the water becoming clearer so that the treasures of the seabed can be discovered.

Deep, deep below on the ocean bed, it remains calm, quiet and peaceful, despite what is happening on the surface.

The ocean is not made of waves – it's made of water – it just has waves.

Just like us!

We're not made of our thoughts - (we're made of approximately 60% water) - we just have thoughts.

Like waves, right around the corner there is another thought waiting to come along. We have these thousands of thoughts each and every day! Out of all these thousands of thoughts, which ones do we hold on to? We don't need to hold onto any of them… there is another one just around the corner.

Great surfers learn about the nature of waves. Before

entering the ocean, they study the surf and identify any hazards or obstacles. They paddle with purpose and choose the perfect moment to surf, so that they can enjoy riding the waves. Either they have been trained, or spent years exploring through experience how to identify the right waves.

Sadly, we weren't born with a manual as to how our thoughts and minds work. We go along life surfing the wrong waves and getting frustrated, putting lots of effect and energy into building these up. These swirl round and round in our minds... and just like the large waves, our minds become cloudy and we feel hurt. And these 'negative' thoughts we have – we make them up! That's the ridiculousness of it all.

The Three Principles are the description (rather than a prescription) of how we work – through **mind**, **consciousness** and **thought**.

The Impact of Understanding

A young client, Gemma, was referred to me by her Mum. She was full of anger. During our coaching she shared that she hated someone from her past. She had hated them for over 10 years and would often focus on this person, believing that they had ruined her life and caused her to have no confidence in herself.

Before coming to me, she had already seen three counsellors over an extended period. Gemma said that during her sessions, all she was doing was reliving her past experiences, reinforcing the hate. She felt angry at the world and that she was the victim.

During our coaching session, I shared with Gemma the wave metaphor and how we don't need to be swallowed up by every wave. Her experiences aren't based on the other person. That person doesn't cause the hate – she is doing that to herself – through her thinking and ultimately, **believing in her thinking**.

We can often get confused, believing that the reality of our experience is based on circumstances outside of us. If that was true – doesn't that mean we are all just puppets? If our feelings and how we experience the world is based on the outside, then what control do we have in our lives? None.

The beauty is that we don't need to try to control or do anything – the thoughts (waves) will just flow right through us if we let them.

Within forty minutes of us talking about this, Gemma

had a new awareness that she was affecting herself with her angry thoughts. The other person had no idea even that she hated them!

It was amazing. She flicked her hand and just let those thoughts go, just like a wave disappearing onto the shoreline – gone forever. And when her thinking was clear, she had a lightbulb moment and could see the treasure within her. What a huge shift. And through having an insight that she wasn't her thoughts – she was so much more than that – awesome!

Having spoken with Gemma recently, from being a very disengaged person in life, she is now thriving, loving her new career, and making waves in peoples' lives.

We all have thousands of thoughts going through our head each day – that's all they are. Thoughts.

I believe that Shakespeare, over 400 years ago, innately knew this:

> *For there is nothing either good or bad, but thinking makes it so.*
> *Hamlet, Act 2, Scene 2, 239–251.*

A thought is a thought is a thought. They keep running through us, all day long. Many are nonsense, often a lot of background noise that we take no notice of.

Since my son has returned home, he often has the radio on. I prefer to work in silence, apart from the noise of the birds chirping. To begin with, I was very consciously aware of the radio, however over time, it began to melt into the background and I no longer take any notice. Occasionally I hear a favourite song and will stop and sing along. Other times a song I dislike is playing. I hear it and then just ignore it, getting on with the task in hand.

And this is exactly the approach you can have with your thoughts. What on earth is the point of listening to thoughts that you perceive to be unhelpful and cruel? It just doesn't make any sense. Thoughts have no meaning: they are neutral. It is us that judges and perceives them as either positive or negative.

When you try and find meaning to your thoughts, analysing them, judging or criticising, searching your history and asking "why?", that's when you end up going round and round in circles, making huge waves, causing massive storms in your mind. All you are doing is adding to your thinking, overthinking.

Just don't do it!

Our thoughts are like Social Media

You may wonder why certain thoughts keep popping up in your consciousness. The content of your thoughts are just like adverts on social media. Think about it – how do these sites such as Facebook decide which adverts you may find interesting and useful? They use the information about you from your social media profile, information you share such as pages you like, your activity via cookies on websites and apps.

Can you see the similarities? I am sure that you don't make a purchase from every social media advert you see and you will certainly not bother even reading an advert that you are not interested in – you would simply ignore or even delete it.

Some thoughts that pop up in our minds can be wonderful to have; I love to reminisce about my Dad who passed away in 2011, his funny idiosyncrasies, happy times we had together and chats we had. I also enjoy having creative thoughts about a new workshop, a client, or writing a blog.

It's the thoughts that are not so useful such as worrying about the future, mindreading what others think about you or being stressed about something out of your control that are not great to hold onto.

Remember that thoughts are neutral; only you can give those thoughts power. The less meaning you give and the less you are engaged with thoughts that are hindering your well-being – the better.

Trust yourself (remember, confidence means 'to have full trust') and let those unhelpful thoughts go.

Our thoughts keep flowing, that's the nature of them. We can let these thoughts slip away, like water through our fingers, without any effort at all. We have a choice as to what we want to focus on. Other than that there is nothing to do: no meditation, no mindfulness, no turning the negative into positive. Another thought will be just round the corner – just like the waves on the ocean!

Chapter 10: What's in the middle of Beliefs?

Aerodynamically the bumblebee shouldn't be able to fly, but the bumblebee doesn't know that so it goes on flying anyway.

MARY KAY ASH

Chapter 10: What's in the middle of Beliefs?

Isn't it funny how we can look at something, sometimes for years, and then one day see it in a different way?

On one of my Confidence Workshops, I wrote the word 'beliefs' in capitals. I stopped and saw it for what it was – a LIE. Look in the middle of the word; it's been there all along!

BE-LIE-FS

Beliefs are all lies – some of them useful, some of them not. *Ok, perhaps I am being a bit facetious!*

What I'm saying here is that beliefs are not facts. Either we borrow beliefs from people who influence us or we make them up – whichever way – they are all created through our own thinking.

All beliefs derive from thought

It has been written many times that fundamental beliefs about ourselves are formed when we are little – in those formative years until we are seven. We might have begun by modelling our parents and 'borrowing' their beliefs – and then the cycle continues. Or perhaps an incident in our past forms a belief that seemed so meaningful at the time. Yet when put into perspective, so meaningless in the bigger scheme of life.

I coached a client who was adamant that she was not good enough. Through coaching, she suddenly remembered that at the age of five she was unable to bunny hop quite as high as her best friend! For years, she had been held back by a feeling of inadequacy based on a brief moment in a playground as a child. When she realised this she was literally crying with laughter, seeing how silly her belief about herself was. It was beautiful to watch her anxieties wash away in that moment.

> *Going back into the past is like going back into the shower to dry off.*
> SYDNEY BANKS

Many people believe that they cannot change their beliefs, including those which may be holding them back. Beliefs such as: "I'm not good enough" or "I'm not confident". They feel that it is so ingrained in them, that it is part of who they are. This is not true.

In addition to the word 'lie', you can find the word 'I' hidden in the middle of 'beliefs'. Our beliefs come from within and have 'I' at the centre. We have ownership of these beliefs. If we learned them, we can unlearn them too, simply by seeing through the lie; the untruths.

Prune your thoughts

Remember, we are flexible, amazing creatures; we have brains that are hyper-plastic. Neuroscience is discovering so much about the brain. Just at the time of writing this, I read a fascinating article about the brain having the ability to let go of old unwanted 'stuff', called 'synaptic pruning'.

Researchers have discovered that synaptic connections that are used infrequently are marked by a protein C1q. When these are detected, glial cells bond to the protein and prune the synapse, allowing our brains additional space for learning. And this all happens when we are asleep!

If you keep having thoughts of old, outdated beliefs... stop it! Take a step back and see them for what they are: lies. Our thoughts are all made up. These beliefs are old stories that you are simply bringing alive through thinking in the moment. Let those limiting thoughts go and allow the brain to expel them naturally.

On one of my Confidence Workshops, a client shared with the group his belief that he didn't have confidence and would spend hours worrying about what others thought about him. When we explored how often this happened, he revealed that some days he would wake up and just get on with life whereas other days he would constantly doubt himself and worry. He recognised that the difference was his thinking at that moment – nothing more, nothing less.

You don't need to understand *why* you have these beliefs (you may never know). Putting any type of analysis onto these beliefs just gives them more form.

You do not need fixing.

These beliefs are just Be-LIE–fs. They are illusionary stories from the past that you have been fuelling and resurrecting, without realising it.

There are plenty of belief change processes and techniques - I used to use these with clients. However these techniques focus on the thoughts giving them power. When we put these beliefs in perspective that they originate from one thought created in one moment, then this weakens the significance. We have the innate wisdom to appreciate our own self-worth and confidence. Without doing a thing!

Leave your old out-of-date stories behind and then your brain will do its magic and overnight those old synapse connections will be deleted, vanished, they will disappear in a puff of smoke... And that is thinking that I have just created in the moment!

Chapter 11: Costs versus Rewards

If you hear a voice within you saying, "You are not a painter," then by all means paint, boy, and that voice will be silenced, but only by working.

VINCENT VAN GOGH - *Letter to Theo van Gogh from Drenthe (October 1883)*

Chapter 11: Costs versus Rewards

So far, I have guided you in the direction of understanding the true nature of us as human beings. That your feelings and experience of life comes from your thoughts (which you make up) and these become real through your consciousness. It seems as if you live in an outside-in world – and that people and situations affect your confidence and you may feel this lowers your self-esteem – however this is all an illusion.

100% of your experience comes from your thinking

Lack of confidence (or should I say obscuring confidence) can affect many areas of our lives: our health, wealth, relationships and productivity, as well as our pure enjoyment of life itself. I hope that you are starting to see that your confidence is a given. It is part of your natural being. The *only* thing that stops you from being confident is your thinking. That is it! Hence – no tips on how to be confident, no techniques and definitely not learning 'how to' change your behaviour... this happens naturally when the cause of your behaviour (thought) changes.

When you are not spending so much energy

ruminating on issues, feeling stressed and getting caught up in your thinking, then all that energy can be used far more productively.

The Sun is always shining somewhere

Obscuring your confidence is simply your thinking clouding your true nature of confidence. The clouds hide the Sun – however the Sun is always there – even during storms, thick fog and the midst of night. The fact is that the Sun is always shining! Nature has a fantastic way of giving us powerful metaphors in life.

Funny, I have been a bit stuck about writing recently and so I just decided to let that go and I knew that my low mood of writing would pass. As if by magic, I have had the urge to write again. I didn't know I was going to write about the Sun, I just did. I have just looked out of my study window to see an amazingly clear blue sky with the sun shining brightly!

The Sun is always there just as our confidence is always there, even beyond the feelings of fear, insecurity, anxiety and low self- esteem. These are all just things that you hold on to unnecessarily. We are living in a thought created experience; we are the thinkers not our thoughts and we can have fresh thought in every moment.

We can see beyond those clouds. They won't stay there forever! By understanding the natural world, we know that the weather system (especially in the UK) rarely stays the same for long. And by understanding the nature of being human, we know that we also rarely stay the same for long.

This obscuring of confidence can affect many areas of your life. Let's explore some of the areas that you may have been struggling with, and see what can happen for you when you appreciate that clarity and confidence are always there...

Chapter 12: Costs versus Rewards – Money

Wealth consists not in having great possessions, but in having few wants.

EPICTETUS

Chapter 12: Costs versus Rewards – Money

Ah, money. This made up way of bartering which seems to have taken over so many people's lives. What is the cost of money? Well, it's not money *per se*. It's the consequences of the anxieties and concerns that people have about this commodity.

Do you spend time focusing on how you can make more money? Do you worry about your bank balance, your income or even your spending rate?

I have experienced all of these in the past. I wasn't paid what I was worth when I was employed and for a long time, I did nothing about this. I believed that I wasn't good enough and would be 'found out'. Even when I set up my coaching business, I would often heavily discount clients and not charge the value of my service.

Setting up your own business does seem a brave step for some people. Strangely, it was a very easy decision for me. Many people presume that if you have the confidence to establish your own business, then you can't possibly lack confidence in yourself. Sadly, this is not true. Many people set up businesses because they are passionate about their products or services. Their wealth is compromised usually for two main reasons: a lack of skills or a perceived 'lack' of confidence.

There are essential skills that must be learnt in order to run your own business: financial acumen, marketing skills, selling and the art of delegating. Failing in any of these areas can cause financial issues if you worry about them, instead of dealing with them from the outset.

However, what I am concentrating on here are the unhelpful beliefs that business owners may have about themselves: things like a fear of rejection, of failure and even of success. Believing that they are not good enough and playing small. Mind reading and being overly concerned about what others think about them. Even feeling needy – which can end up repelling rather than attracting people.

Steve's Story

Let me introduce you to Steve. Steve was struggling to earn enough money in his business so it felt like a big decision for him to invest in coaching (albeit a wise one). He was spending a huge amount of his time worrying about the business which was impacting his level of confidence, triggering a downward spiral. Steve was on the point of giving up and throwing in the towel, but there was something inside him that was stopping him. He recognised that many business owners give up, even though they are passionate and full of talent. Their confidence issues and clouded thinking caused their businesses to fail and he didn't want to be yet another statistic.

Steve agreed that in the past, when he was in a low mood, he would worry about money and the consequences that it could have on his future and that of his family. He shared that in his imaginary thinking; he'd loose the family home and end up on the streets and so on.

When he was in a high mood, money wasn't an issue; he enjoyed networking, spending time on his business, with his clients. Reflecting on this, he appreciated that he wasn't focusing on money – it wasn't even in the equation of his thinking! And what's more, those moments of enjoyment were when he noticed that more business opportunities came his way.

Since our coaching session, Steve saw an opportunity to diversify his business, which has started to reap financial rewards for him. He also noticed that things that would have caused him stress in the past, he is now able to deal with very calmly with a *laissez faire* attitude. He used to be busy trying to change his thinking – actively attempting to change negative thoughts into positive ones, and now, he just isn't caught up in his thoughts. He feels calmer and able to deal with situations easier now. The result is that he is richer, calmer, more productive and enjoying working in and on his business.

Confidence issues also have financial ramifications for those who are employed. Doubts surrounding self-deprecation and the inability to see their own worth can result in people not applying for promotions and even shying away from demonstrating their worth at appraisal times. The impact is that they can miss out on bonuses and pay increases.

Peter's Story

I was working with a wonderfully talented client, Peter, whose job was redundant. In one of our early sessions I challenged him about playing small. He was applying for jobs that were grades below his capability following his redundancy. Peter admitted that his confidence had taken a serious knock. When I shared with him the nature of mind, consciousness and thought, he confessed that it wasn't the redundancy at all that was affecting him. In fact, he hadn't enjoyed his previous job anyway! He had been listening to his 'small' thoughts and started to believe them.

The shift was liberating. His mood lifted and he started remembering examples of where he had made positive impacts in previous jobs. He identified the essence of what was unique about him: his knowledge, skills and strengths. With his renewed confidence, he got out and networked and was soon offered a fantastic position with a salary £10,000 more than those he was previously looking at. Peter loves his new role – a pretty good rate of return from having just a few coaching sessions!

Homeless and Happy?

Now you may be thinking – well, great for people that have money. What if you don't have any money, you are on benefits or even worse, homeless? Surely you would be worrying then. Knowing and understanding the principles of thought, of confidence, of peace of mind, doesn't put food on the table or a roof over your head, does it?

Let me introduce you to a man called Race C Calmer. He is in his early 60s and moved up to London to find work. I noticed him (he was rather hard to miss!) as he was stood on the pavement holding a large brightly coloured notice board that read, "Don't worry, be happy and smile because you are amazing". We had a quick chat and then I went on my way.

As time passed by, I kept thinking about Race and wondered what his story was. How could he be homeless and happy?

I had taken a photo of him and his board and when I found that he had a Facebook page, I was compelled to connect with him and read his story. Race came from a broken home, a bit of a scoundrel and had spent much of his life in and out of prison. Not something he was proud of. *Humans of London* interviewed Race and they have both given me permission to share part of the interview:

At first, when I came up here from Portsmouth, I was using my sign to try and get a job, but that wasn't working. Then I had a dream where everyone was smiling, instead of looking miserable or staring at their phones, and I realised that this is what I should do, this is what I'm here for. So I did a new sign which said 'Smile because you are you!' Then, on my 61st birthday, some girls from an office round here got me some colour felt tips and my artistic manoeuvres came out. I never asked for money, I never begged in my life. I'm just showing off my artwork and the board always looks after me. I've never wanted for anything, I've never gone hungry, and I sleep in a little pop-up tent hidden in St James's Park. Nobody knows I'm there and I respect the park because it's St James's Park – I could be at one of the spots where Henry the Eighth proposed to one of his queens or shot his first deer! I don't have any friends, just acquaintances on the street and in the cafés, but I'm never lonely because I'm happy in myself. I'm a lone wolf and I'm fine with that because now I'm in touch with my soul and I've found my purpose in life.

Wow! How amazing is that? When I reflect on this, Race now has such wisdom… what a change from his past. It's not the outside environment that 'makes' him feel happy, or sad, or lonely. He has sensed that his feelings come from himself. He is the master of his own mind!

So remember, it's not money that 'makes' us unconfident, worried or stressed. That is the illusionary outside-in thinking. Money cannot make you be confident or feel happy. Our moods and feelings change our experience and view of our world. If we are in a low mood then it probably isn't the best time to make big dramatic decisions about money! Many of those 'get rich quick' schemes are for those who are desperate. Believe me, I have spent a lot of time in the past thinking that if I go on this course or that course, then that will turn my income around. I attended some of them but it didn't work. I still had the same insecure thinking.

Allow those clouds unsettling your mind to just blow away and you will soon experience that your confidence is always there, shining bright!

The Reward

As you begin to enjoy what you have and stop worrying about the money and things you don't have, you can enjoy life and live more in the moment. Refraining from worrying about money means that you will naturally become more resourceful, have more energy and be clear minded.

Steve, Peter and Race don't worry about money now. They have inner confidence and trust, and the result is that they are enjoying life far more.

The rewards? You will have the mind space to have amazing insights and you may find that new opportunities open up for you...

Chapter 13: Costs versus Rewards – Time

The only reason for time is so that everything doesn't happen at once...

RAY CUMMINGS *1921 short story 'The Time Professor'*

Chapter 13: Costs versus Rewards – Time

Self-doubt and obscuring confidence definitely costs time. I can certainly vouch for that!

Do you take ages to do tasks or keep putting things off? Do you have items on your 'to do' list that have been on there for weeks – if not months? What is the reason for this? Why are you putting off achieving these tasks? Is it because they are not important? (If so, just remove them from your list.) Or are you procrastinating, avoiding the issue? Are you spending more time and energy stressing over what needs to be done, instead of just getting on with doing it? Do you doubt yourself? Lack of confidence costs you time – through either procrastinating or being a perfectionist.

Kay was a business owner and had set up her own agency. She came to me for a coaching session as she kept procrastinating and avoiding picking up the phone to call potential clients. This was having a negative effect on her business which she wanted to grow. She had the skills – she was just putting off using them for fear of failure.

Through guiding her in the direction of the nature of

thought and feelings, Kay rediscovered her love for her business and approached it in a more positive manner. I called her a few weeks later and she said that she was already seeing the results, easily and effortlessly calling up companies and converting them into clients.

Her procrastination and lack of confidence was all in her thinking – she was caught up with doubt and the fear of being rejected.

Procrastinating via Perfectionism

Procrastination is often a by-product of being a perfectionist. Years ago, a friend was telling me about his business and how he was taking ages to set up a website as he wanted it to be perfect – and labelled himself as a perfectionist. I immediately said to him "perfectionism is just an excuse not to get things done." Even to this day, he often tweets my quote on Twitter – it obviously made an impact on him.

The reason I said this to him was that I used to be a perfectionist, triggered by my perceived lack of confidence at the time. When I worked in the finance industry I would work ridiculously long hours. When I resigned, the cleaner and security guard both gave me leaving presents as they knew me so well! I would often be working until midnight, wanting to get things perfect. Even a two page report would take me hours to write. I would go over and over it again and again, tweaking, changing... argh! It was painful. Perhaps you can relate to this?

If you think about a flower at its most perfect – what happens next? It dies. So if we ever manage to be perfect, how boring would life be afterwards? There would be nothing left to learn.

Sometimes we just need to be 'good enough'. When we aren't consumed in our thinking and fully trust ourselves, things just seem to flow. Like me sitting here in my office, writing my book. I am allowing the words to stream out of my consciousness... I am sure that they are good enough – not perfect – and that is fine.

Feeling stuck

Annie had been referred to me by two networking friends and decided it was about time she listened to them. She came to me for coaching as she was feeling stuck. Something was holding her back from making progress on a new business project. She didn't know what the something was, or what to do about it. She was becoming pretty negative about the project and the effect was that her confidence was waning.

In our coaching session, we didn't once talk about the business project. Annie shared that she was going round in circles and she felt that a number of past events had left her feeling stuck.

That morning before our coaching session, during my usual morning walk, a memory popped up in my head of when my husband and I had our first flat together.

We had purchased a new sofa and when the delivery men arrived, they insisted that the sofa would not get up the stairs of our flat. Ten minutes later, they hoisted it up through a window... but into the wrong room.

I remembered how we attempted to move the sofa ourselves. We got it through the first doorway, shuffled it round the hallway and then... it was stuck. We shoved and pushed, we heaved and tugged but the sofa would just not get through that doorway. After getting thoroughly hot, sweaty and frustrated my husband suggested we stopped and, in typical

English style, we had a cup of tea, dunking our biscuits and gradually calming down. Once we were refreshed, we had another go. One small nudge and hey presto, the sofa easily moved into the room.

I shared that story with my client, Annie.

The coaching session gave her breathing space, allowing her to have insights. We explored what was happening to her. It wasn't about past events, it wasn't about the project – it was how she was thinking about the issues. Moreover, it was that she had believed her thinking. And her thinking affected how she was feeling.

Once Annie understood the mechanics of her thinking, the tension and stress on her face melted away and she looked 10 years younger. Honestly! It was beautiful... and of course, we celebrated with a nice cup of tea.

> *My mind and confidence have been much clearer since that first meeting and people have noticed and told me so! My confidence has returned...*

We can all get stuck from time to time. I occasionally feel stuck when I am writing this book. What a paradox! So I let go of thinking about writing, have a cup of tea and then sit back down and allow the writing to flow...

An Exercise for You

I know I promised that this book wouldn't involve exercises and techniques, but I would like to break my own rules, just for a moment.

What I would like you to do is to take a break. Step away from this book and get yourself a drink... a cup of tea, a coffee, perhaps a gin and tonic! Whatever your tipple is. Now hold the mug (or glass) out in front of you without leaning your arm or elbow on anything – go on – stick it right out.

How heavy is the mug? Not too heavy? I've just weighed mine and it is 567 grams. Carry on reading whilst holding your arm straight out. How long do you think that you can keep your arm out before the mug seems to become too heavy? As you know, it still weighs the same (unless you have been sneakily drinking from it). However your upper arm and shoulder will start to ache, the muscles start to judder and the pain increases. Ouch! I hope you still have your arm stretched out...

If you want the pain to stop – what will you do? Put the mug down. Simple.

It's just like our thoughts. When we hold onto them for a long time or they are stuck – it hurts. All we need to do is to put them down, to let go.

When we are stuck because of a problem at work, issues at home or in a relationship, and feeling emotionally stuck – this feeling stuck seeps into other areas of our life and seems that it can affect our confidence, our stress levels and our productivity. It's like we dig ourselves deeper and deeper into the mire of despair.

These feelings of 'being stuck' are all an illusion. When we identify that we created the stuck feelings ourselves, that's when the magic happens and we can free ourselves from this torment. Problems cannot be solved with the same kind of thinking that created them.

As Hilary Mantel says:

> *If you get stuck, get away from your desk. Take a walk, take a bath, go to sleep, make a pie, draw, listen to music, meditate, exercise; whatever you do,*

don't just stick there scowling at the problem. But don't make telephone calls or go to a party; if you do, other people's words will pour in where your lost words should be. Open a gap for them, create a space. Be patient.

The Rewards

Can you see the rewards that understanding the Three Principles bring? Personally, I have noticed a huge difference in the value of my time. I manage to get on with things without lingering on them. As a matter of fact, it is 7:34am on a Sunday morning as I type this. I woke up and decided to make a couple of tweaks to this book so I just got on with it, effortlessly. In the past I would have stayed in bed and gone through the changes in my head for ages, before I actually managed to get them done. What a waste of energy!

I have so much more energy these days. Little things like clearing up, replying to emails or going for a walk, they just happen. I now have more time without using any special time management techniques (which I never found worked anyway) and I hope that you will notice the same!

A caveat: It may not happen immediately. When I first discovered the Three Principles, I heard many people enthuse that they had so much more energy. For me, the opposite happened! Sometimes I felt tired and would even have a nap in an afternoon – something that I very rarely did. Looking back, I think I needed the down time. Remember that we are all different so please, just go with the flow, and see what happens over time.

Chapter 14: Costs versus Rewards – Relationships

In a healthy state we are like Dr. Jekyll. When we lose this state, hello Mr. Hyde. Mr. and Mrs. Jekyll always have a good marriage. Mr. and Mrs. Hyde always have problems. It takes only one Jekyll to move a marriage towards health.
GEORGE PRANSKY. *The Relationship Handbook*

Chapter 14: Costs versus Rewards – Relationships

What is the cost in terms of relationships? I'm not just talking about relationships with others, but also with yourself. The cost of not feeling confident is huge. It affects your own well-being, and with others can create friction, conflict, bullying behaviour and in the context at work, lack of success.

Business and work aren't just about processes, products and services, marketing strategies, finance. I would say that in all businesses and life in general, the most important thing is relationships – with colleagues, partners, clients, suppliers, and friends as well as of course our family. If relationships are not good then this will affect morale and productivity.

I am currently working with a company and one of the directors shared that he spends much of his time sorting out internal conflict amongst his employees. What a waste of energy and time! Not to mention that it can't be a particularly pleasant environment for people to work in if they are constantly nit-picking, blaming each other or worse – bullying.

Of course it is imperative to have good relationships

with clients. No clients mean no business. It's also important to have great relationships with suppliers. They can really help you out when things go wrong! I remember a print supplier once pulling out all the stops for me – way beyond all expectation – simply because we had such a great relationship together.

Now this all seems obvious. However your confidence can really affect the quality of relationships both within work and outside of work. If you label yourself as shy, then perhaps attending meetings or networking events feels difficult. Your nervousness causes you to hesitate and you may avoid speaking out – even though you have some great ideas. There are so many potential scenarios; I could write a whole book just describing them! But for now, it's more important to see that all of the issues arise because of the illusions surrounding how we think. I did say that I would be repeating myself now, didn't I?

The most important relationship to focus on and build is with yourself. How can you possibly have good relationships with others if you don't with yourself? You will come across as a fraud and people will quickly see through this.

Often we want to fit in so we mould ourselves to whatever group we are with, be it family, work, various networks, old school friends, neighbours. We become like a chameleon, changing the way we look, speak and act; wanting to be liked and assuming that we have to be a certain way. Or we may feel that we never fit in, the outsider, always feeling like the oddball, a bit different and never getting particularly close to anyone.

What I have appreciated now is that it wasn't the groups or the other people that made me feel awkward. It was what was going on in my head. People can like me, or not! Since I have let go of my insecure and self-doubting thoughts I feel completely comfortable with a whole range of people and groups. Isn't that what we all want?

When we get over ourselves, don't treat ourselves so seriously and preciously, life becomes so much easier, more fun, light hearted and effortless. And the simplicity of this is that there really is nothing to do. No tips, no techniques, no analysis, no doubts, no judgement. Just love, a sense of freedom, peace, becoming grounded, feeling more open, compassionate and grateful.

Jenny came to see me as she was feeling deeply unhappy with life. In our first session, she shared how she tried so hard to be liked, often going out of her way for others. This sounded nice, however she admitted that she was now feeling quite resentful doing this. She was unconsciously playing the drama triangle game – sometimes acting as a rescuer, then getting fed up and persecuting, then because people didn't want to be with her, she played the victim game. I sensed that this had been going on for years.

It struck me that Jenny's thoughts of herself were very harsh. It was as if she needed to have outside love because she didn't love herself. Slowly over time, Jenny started to see that she was hurting herself with her own made-up thinking. Most of this was habitual. It was like an addiction. At first she even started feeling anxious about being at peace! What would she do with herself? She was so conditioned to overthink and say cruel things to herself it seemed alien to do otherwise. And then she would mentally beat herself up even more. It was becoming a vicious circle, which Jenny did eventually manage to break (back to this shortly!).

Addictive Thinking

When someone says addiction, we usually assume that they will be talking about addictions to alcohol, drugs or gambling. Why do people become addicted to these? Usually because the person believes that the 'thing' makes them feel better. It doesn't! When you are not high on the effects of the addiction, then you almost always come back down to earth with a bump. These extreme highs and lows often become addictive themselves.

There are other less obvious addictions such as overthinking, being busy and self-critical thoughts, which many people suffer from. Addictions are due to a pattern of thinking that arises when you want to feel a different way. People get addicted to something because in that short moment in time, it seems as if they feel better or it takes the pain away. As the 'drug' wears off, they revert to the pattern of thinking they want to avoid and so it repeats, eventually becoming habitual.

The principles give us the ability to have new perspectives – it's like we can be detached from our thinking and see the nature of thought. Our thoughts seem real, however we are living in our very own created experience, brought to life by these principles. Our own thinking (including our beliefs about ourselves) is the only thing that gets in our way.

Coming back to Jenny, it was a gradual shift for her, not a whizz-bang transformational enlightenment! She woke up one day and recognised that she had been feeling very calm inside for a number of days and it seemed that she hadn't 'done' anything. She had started enjoying her own company more and didn't feel the need to always be entertaining people and doing things to gain acknowledgement. She was feeling happier in her own skin, being kinder to herself and wasn't second-guessing about other people or mind reading so much.

Can you Mind Read?

Imagine this scenario:

You are sitting in a room in a group of people from all different backgrounds. What links them is that they are all interested in learning. Gradually, one by one, they share what they want to achieve from this time together. One of them is sitting there looking uncomfortable. A slight pink deepens on their face and they look down to the ground, avoiding eye contact. What is going on in their head is this:

"They were all expecting loads from me and now they are wondering why I am here – I feel such a fraud – in fact they think I am a fraud. I feel so stupid. They all think I'm stupid. Argh I am stupid… Oh, I wish the floor could swallow me up."

And the thoughts carry on – as the person mind reads what the others are thinking. If you think about it – mind reading is such an amazing skill. To be able to sit there and mind read what other people are thinking… wow! What a talent! *Yes – my tongue is in cheek as I write this!*

Are you a mind reader? The above is the typical inner dialogue that I had before I discovered the Three Principles – when I experienced a period of doubt and insecurity. At a Confidence Workshop earlier this year one of the participants got up and walked out of the room to get a drink. In my head I decided that she wasn't engaged in the workshop and I started to feel concerned. A moment later I recognised I had been hoodwinked by the illusion of my thinking. I shared this with the group and we all had a good laugh at the ridiculousness of my thinking!

Perhaps you get anxious about what others think about you and then make up stories in your head – belittling yourself and worrying about your body image or intelligence. Are other people really spending all their time thinking about you? I doubt it! I mentioned this to a client and she burst out laughing (my clients and I often have a good laugh, I do think we can take ourselves too seriously at times and laughter is a great healer). She suddenly had an insight and realised how egotistical she was being:

"It's all about me! I thought that everyone was spending their precious time thinking about me! Wow that is so self-centred."

I loved her sense of humour and how she fondly mocked herself. After our coaching, she shared with me:

"I have become more confident and no longer worry about what a person's opinion may or may not be about me. Unless they actually tell me, I have absolutely no idea. I now can't wait to start my next chapter in my life."

This egotistical tendency to mind read causes so much unnecessary worry and anxiety... and it's becoming an epidemic. It is all an illusion and *all made up!* We see something that isn't there and make it personal – we believe others are thinking about us, when they may even be thinking that we are thinking about them! We are turning ourselves into puppets, allowing the outside world to pull our emotional strings. Let's stop this epidemic and snap those strings.

You may have noticed the trickery of your own thinking in certain circumstances and that, of course, you cannot actually mind read. (Though please do let me know if you can!) Now you may be wondering how to stop mind reading and worrying. Am I right?

Do you remember that in Chapter 7 I mentioned that we have over 70,000 thoughts in a day? They are like waves in the ocean, flowing through, yet only some of those many thoughts ping into our consciousness. The problems arise when we:

a) Believe that the outside world 'makes' us feel a certain way.
b) Feed our thoughts and build them up to an almighty crescendo.

The thinking is not the problem! After all, we are

thinkers, we always have thoughts and we always will. Thought is just a tool – that's it – an amazing tool to direct us through life, to allow us to have human experience. So use it wisely and please, *don't take it too seriously!*

Relationships with Others

What about our relationships with others? If we are living in our own thought-created experience, then we can appreciate that so is everyone else!

Issues in relationships often arise because:

- We think others see things the same way as us and then become intolerant when they react differently to us.
- We think that others should see things the way we do – we're right and they are wrong. We believe that we see reality the real way.

We all have a different perspective on life. It's not surprising! We have all had different upbringings and even amongst our siblings, we will have different memories of our childhoods.

Last year I was with my two wonderful sisters and we were reminiscing about our younger days. I mentioned an incident when our Mum found a pencil mark on the fridge door. She went ballistic! We were due to go out that afternoon to visit friends of our parents who I was very fond of, and our Mum said we would only go once one of us admitted to making the pencil mark. Now, this pencil mark really was just a pencil mark – it wasn't a drawing – just a mark that someone may have inadvertently done if they were waving a pencil around when they passed the fridge door.

I can picture it now... Or can I? I think I can, however, is this my own thought in the moment remembering a memory of remembering a memory from over 45 years ago? Who knows!

I digress... Going back to my sisters and me recalling this occasion, one of my sisters didn't know what I was talking about and couldn't remember it at all. My other sister had a different version of the event entirely!

Even though we are sisters and were present at the same event, our perceptions and memories of it are totally different.

The realisation that each thought system is different

deepened for me recently. I was at a concert at the Corn Exchange in Cambridge listening to KT Tunstall. The Victorian building is perfect for a concert, with its beautiful high ceiling.

While listening to the music, I (for no apparent reason), starting thinking about my Mum. I then had a powerful insight; every person in the audience was experiencing the concert in their own unique way. No one else was sitting there thinking about my Mum – now that would have been weird! We were all at the same gig, in the same venue, listening to the same music and yet every single one of us was experiencing it differently. I found this incredible.

We all have individual thought systems – our backgrounds, memories, circumstances and mood levels are all different. So of course, our thinking is different even though we may be in the same room as another person. Based on this, it's surprising that we understand each other at all! Perhaps we don't?

We are all unique... even twins. When we fully expect that others will have different thoughts and therefore react differently to ourselves, then we can come from a place of compassion, curiosity and let go of always having to 'be right'. When this happens, conflict and quarrels can be eradicated. What a different world it would be.

The Rewards

This new awareness of our relationships (be it in our business or personal life) means that we can be free from relationship problems. It is impossible to see fully how another person experiences the world – there are too many variables. Instead, through appreciating that we all have unique thought systems, we can enjoy and be curious about people's differences. We can respect their viewpoints. When that happens people don't get defensive – they connect and have more fulfilling relationships. They will sense your innate confidence and build trust in you.

You don't need to compare yourself to others or mind read. Can you see that through respecting the differences between people, you don't need to be right or wrong and can be perfectly comfortable with this? You no longer need to be concerned about what others are thinking of you (mind reading). All those insecure feelings come from your insecure thinking... just an illusion. Do you really need to be insecure now?

Confidence is there – that gentle truth that we are all doing our best, having insights, connecting with others. Since coming across the Three Principles I have on purpose spent time with people who I once used to struggle with. My barriers and shields have dropped, and I am suddenly able to build wonderful, meaningful relationships with them. Who do you struggle with? What if you were curious and wanted to get to know them? See what happens for you.

Rediscovering your confidence in yourself and building respect for others brings a grounded-ness, openness and lightness. All of which are far more attractive than blaming, arguing or avoiding others. This enables you to have new opportunities and a deep connection with yourself and others.

Got it? Enjoy!

Chapter 15: Costs versus Rewards – Health

When you have a bruise, do you go poking at it to heal it?
GEORGE PRANSKY

Chapter 15: Costs versus Rewards – Health

Issues with confidence can often affect your health, both physically and mentally. At what cost? By constantly doubting yourself and having low self-esteem, many people begin to feel anxious, stressed and continuously worried. Over time, this can have a detrimental effect on their health.

Are your confidence problems costing you sleep? Not sleeping well can increase the risk of serious medical conditions such as obesity, heart disease, high blood pressure and diabetes.

One of my clients popped over as she wanted support with a challenging decision that she needed to make. Amongst other things, we talked about the Three Principles, trust and tapping into our own wisdom.

At a subsequent networking meeting she gave me a wonderful testimonial and shared with the group that she had suffered from a lack of sleep for years. She announced that since our session she is now sleeping soundly every night. We didn't even talk about sleep once during our session!

Are your confidence issues costing you your

happiness or preventing you from leading the life that you rightly deserve? Are they costing you success – perhaps you are playing small but deep down you know you are capable of more?

Constant negative thoughts have the power to cause tension in your body. This can affect your breathing (it is amazing how many people actually breathe in quite a damaging way), which can increase adrenaline levels and cause chemical imbalances in your body. These sensations can result in further feelings of anxiety, triggering a rapid downward spiral.

A few years ago, I suddenly woke up in the middle of the night and had an intense feeling of anxiety. The whole of my body was rigid, I was sweating profusely, my skin was tingling, I felt uncomfortable, and my mind hurt. It was overwhelming. Why was I feeling so anxious? Yes, I had teenage children, my own business, a mortgage to pay, my Mum was ill (we can all think of something to feel anxious about if we set our minds that way) but these sensations were far too strong. Ah! I was a lady of a certain age… it was my hormones playing havoc… and I went back to sleep.

I didn't know about the Three Principles at that time, but whether we know about them or not, they still exist. I just had a sense that there wasn't anything to be concerned about.

I personally believe that illness arises because of 'dis-ease' within us. I know that in the past, when I was extremely stressed at work, as soon as I had a break I would become ill. It was as if my body was saying "enough is enough". Our bodies are like our own messenger highlighting the condition of our mental well-being.

What about if you do have an illness or medical condition? Going back to when I woke up in the middle of the night feeling anxious, I could have labelled myself menopausal. These labels are not very useful as they become a focal point and can even become part of our identity.

Do you label yourself?

"I am bipolar" "I am depressed" "I am dyslexic" "I am shy" and so on. You are not any of these labels. If a person has cancer – they are not cancer. They have an illness called cancer. Now don't get me wrong, I am not belittling this by any means. You don't need to own any label nor allow them to overtake your life.

Cancer and Depression

Wendi Saggese was diagnosed with Cancer in 2010 and it totally consumed her and her family's life. Having to deal with the illness, deciding what treatment to have, the pressure of being a mum to her two children, and knowing that she may die, was traumatic for her. She felt like a victim to her circumstance of having cancer and couldn't focus on anything else in her life apart from the cancer.

Luckily, Wendi came across the Three Principles and since understanding these, her whole experience of her condition has changed. She realised that the circumstance of cancer wasn't causing her to feel a certain way; it was her thinking about it. Now she has more joy in life and feels a sense of freedom. She is living again. Yes, she still has cancer; however she doesn't label herself with this condition now. She is far more than cancer. And now she is helping others who are suffering from illness to live with ease.

I personally suffered from post-natal depression after having my second child. I remember the feeling of a huge black cloud over my head, the numbness, the lethargy and sense of hopelessness. Feeling that I wasn't good enough as a Mum or as a Project Manager at work, I wanted to shut off from the world.

What I was doing was constantly reminding myself that I was depressed, and then of course I was; this becomes the reality of our thinking.

Sometimes when people feel this way it can seem impossible to escape. *It is possible.* Depression isn't 24/7. It may come in waves or be better during certain times of day. A close friend suffered with depression however she was better in the afternoon than first thing in the morning. I noticed that she found it difficult to deal with future situations, she would instantly imagine that she wouldn't be able to cope – even though often these events were months away.

As with me, there was probably a chemical imbalance. It wasn't just that I was tired from having two young children and working. Yet now I see that it all stemmed from my thinking, being caught up and believing the drivel that was running through my head. The consequence of this constant angst often becomes clinical depression.

When you notice where your feelings are coming from (your thinking) then you don't need to focus on the content. Let me recap, you are a thinker and not your thoughts, so by not getting caught up and allowing yourself to let go, it is amazing how quickly your mind clears.

Do you remember from Chapter 1 that up until the 18th century people believed that disease came from bad smells? Yes, those smells were an indicator, but that wasn't the place to look for the answer. It is the same with your feelings – they are indicators of your thinking, they are not the cause.

You still have innate mental well-being – it's there, underneath all that noise in your head, deep inside of you, in your soul. It is in your blue print, you were born that way and it will never disappear!

I share this because *I care about you*. We may not have ever met, however I care. I believe that people don't need to suffer from mental illness – I have experienced mental illness myself and watched people very close to me suffer. By having a deeper awareness of the principles of being human, it changes everything.

The Rewards

The Three Principles are not something that we use, or a step-by-step guide. They are simply basic truths behind our psychological experience. The clearer we see how something works, the more effectively we can use it; be it a machine, our bodies or our minds.

When we throw off the shackles trapping ourselves in our heads, the newfound liberation gives us a huge boost in our mental wellbeing, health and quality of life.

Got it? I hope that by now you are starting to experience:

- A natural feeling of confidence
- Clear mindedness, peace and clarity
- Making decisions easier
- Enjoying life from a sense of lightness
- More energy, resulting in being effectively productive
- Overcoming any anxieties or conflicts quickly and effortlessly

What a great reward from living via these simple Three Principles! Go out and live a confident, productive and stress-free life.

Got it! A Synopsis

I don't want to appear overconfident.

Over-confidence is an oxymoron. Overly confident behaviour is just a distraction so that vulnerabilities are hidden.

The true meaning of confidence is to have full trust. With this inner confidence and trust means that whatever happens in life, you will get through it.

How do I overcome suffering from lack of confidence?

It seems that you are lacking in confidence, however the truth is that we all have confidence – it is part of our blueprint. It's just that insecure thinking hides your confidence. Through understanding the principles of all human experience you will rediscover your confidence.

What are the principles of all human experience?

These are called the Three Principles (Mind, Consciousness and Thought) which were discovered by Sydney Banks and point to the true nature of the human experience.

In his words:

> *Mind* is the universal intelligence behind life, *Consciousness* creates an awareness of what we call reality, and *Thought* is the power to create our moment to moment existence.

Who was Sydney Banks?

Sydney Banks was a very ordinary man, a Scottish welder who moved to Canada. He had a spiritual enlightened experience where he recognised the source of all suffering and all healing. This knowledge has been alluded to over thousands of years however the simplistic way Sydney shared the Three Principles has enabled people to grasp how the mind works via the description of the nature of the human experience. The impact of this knowledge is that it changes lives; people are more confident, productive and stress-free.

How can this help me feel confident?

Through understanding the Three Principles, we can see that our whole experience in life comes from our thoughts rather than the outside world. There are three key points to this:

a) Our experience is 'inside-out'. Our experience of life 100% of the time depends on the type of thought or feeling we are having in the moment. If we feel insecure (impacting our confidence levels), this totally comes from our insecure thinking which we have created in that moment. We make it up!

b) We are thinkers, not our thoughts, and we create new thinking in any moment. We have thousands of thoughts each day so there is no point in holding on to our made up thoughts that don't support us.

c) The nature of who we are is that we have innate wisdom, intelligence and confidence. When we get out of our heads and our made up thinking, and trust ourselves, then things tend to work out for the best.

How else will this understanding impact me?

Let me ask you a question. How much time do you spend worrying? Overthinking? Mind reading? Are you doing this monthly? Weekly? Daily? A lot?

Imagine having all that time and energy spare. Wow – how will that feel for you?

It is as if a huge weight will be lifted from your shoulders. You will find that you are so much more productive with a sense of lightness; you will be more comfortable with other people – whoever they are. Even in the face of adversity, you aren't caught up in any perceived drama. Life seems easier, effortless and with a sense of joy. I do hope that you've got it!

What Next?

If you wish to learn more at a deeper level, then below is some further reading for you:

- Enlightened Gardner – Sydney Banks

- The Missing Link – Sydney Banks

- Nuggets of Wisdom – Elsie Spittle

- Our True Identity – Elsie Spittle

- Somebody Should Have Told Us! – Jack Pransky

- The Relationship Handbook – George Pransky

- The Space Within – Michael Neill

About the Author

Welcome, I am Lindsey Reed, a Confidence Coach who has been professionally coaching clients around the world since 2005. I also facilitate many workshops based on the Three Principles; both open workshops as well as within businesses and the public sector. My aim is to touch millions of people's lives so they recognise and become their extra-ordinariness. Currently living in the UK with my wonderful husband, we have two amazing grown up sons.

I hope that you have enjoyed and benefitted from reading this book. Connect and share your journey with me on the Glows Coaching Facebook page or Twitter @GlowsCoaching. It would be great to see a photo of you with the book, showing that you have 'Got It!'

For information about coaching sessions, workshops, or speaking engagements please contact me at: lindsey@glows-coaching.co.uk.

And Thanks...

There are a number of key people who have had a major impact on helping me write this book, some people directly and some indirectly. A huge thank you to Laura Davies who has proof read, edited and helped with designing the book, such a multi-talented lady.

Also thanks to Andy Bolt, Catherine de Salvo, Cathy Teesdale, Elsie Spittle, George Pransky, George Reed, Georgia Wilkinson, Helen Askey, Jac Gardner, John Reed, Karen Williams, Keith Blevens, Kim Bennett, Michael Neill, Race C Calmer, Rachel Barnes, Rachel Parrott, Sam Pearce, Simon Gardner, Tim Reed, and Wendi Saggese. I feel blessed being connected with such generous and supportive people.

Thank you to all the clients I have connected with and learnt from over the years. And especially to those who have very kindly given me permission to include their experiences in this book (some names are changed for confidentiality).

I very much appreciate Sara Lazar, PhD, Neuroscientist of Yoga and Meditation at Massachusetts General Hospital and Harvard

Medical School and Professor Jerome Kagan PhD, Daniel and Amy Starch Research Professor of Psychology at Harvard University for giving me permission to include their studies of Meditation and Child Behaviour respectively.

Over the years I've had many amazing teachers who have supported me with my own development, including Kevin Cherry, Curly Martin, Sue Knight, Kimberley Hare and many more.

And my biggest teacher is Tim Reed. In all these years, he is the essence of what I had been searching for.

Lightning Source UK Ltd.
Milton Keynes UK
UKOW05f0615300317
297891UK00018B/576/P